A BODY OF POEMS

a body of poems

Jane Covernton

Calendula Farms
Vancouver
2007

Library and Archives Canada Cataloguing in
Publication

Covernton, Jane, 1949-
        A body of poems / Jane Covernton.

ISBN 978-1-4303-2590-1

        I. Title.

PS8555 O8524 B63 2007   C811'.54
C2007-906044-7

Published by
Calendula Farms
1296 East 17th Ave., Vancouver, B.C. Canada V5V 1C6
janeco@vcn.bc.ca

for John, Carl, Reynaldo, Tom, Lib, Daphne,

& *for my parents Carl and Betty*
(may their souls rest in peace)

contents

One:
The city is holy

Unrecorded Dreams

Even the therapist won't listen anymore because I haven't been
doing the work
I get to the lodge but the writers have all gone on ahead. I go
out to continue up the mountain but have to go back because it's
getting dark. I have the black bounding optimist dog. I don't
know how I'll get down the mountain through dark wet bushes.
I don't even have a flashlight.
      A man comes to guide me.

This is about wilderness slipping away in dreams, about being
wireless, unconnected. It is about the
   body,
      hands holding paper books, things that are rough to the
hand. Like borage, comfrey.
Things that are rough to the hand, that smell good, getting to
know trees by their bark,
Douglas fir resin brilliant
 sticky on the hand.
Down by the lake Cottonwood buds issue balm after high wind.
This is being written in haste, a message out of silence, a small
door open.

This is a polemic against virtual reality, against words, against
movies, against the Net, against Toronto, against TV, against
cars, against perfume, against advertising, against Aids, against
fear, against being Online All the Time, against voice-mail.

This is about dis-ease. Someone said, quoting someone, (I read
it somewhere): poets don't drive. I drive around and around the
city,

11

dripping oil, tracing my
        body on the known routes,
It's how I garden too: around and around the known routes
        in rain, early darkness, anger in the chrome air across
the dripping laurel hedge.
Too many people, pressure, we're evolving as fast as we can.

This is about sex, old lady sex, sexy old lady, long grey hair
loose on the wind. In the meantime, every breath in this house
has my name on it.

This is about sex and poetry and things that smell
  on the hand
sex is the one real thing, two skins talking.

like a shell

men's hands wash over me
and my colours fade.

- 1976

A Perfect Love

Outside a sudden April summer
   surprised we go sleeveless
inside the bus: one Buddhist book, no choice.

per-mission, this flowing through, this exchange of information.

no choice and unexpected exchange in enforced intimacy
bare elbows touch
I could
   fold my arms and lean away, legs tight.
And you could too.
But Globe and Mail slips down your lap
   I sleep

and lucid dream:
our rubbing skin
      that elbow patch
you unafraid
open, like me, into arm skin speeches of soft endearment
not insistent.

I stir and fold lap-slid paper,
stand, lift down coat:
soft black London wool
for chilled blur window-side,
open Buddha book,
and doze awake.

you were reading A Handmaid's Tale, but in this world
   dozing trees blur by.

I like your mind but it doesn't matter.
no seduction, no loss, no means no.
your arm fits under mine
but know: no heads off-chopt
          what if he doesn't like me?
start where you are:
          love is not dangerous here
your arm quiet against my chest
          my side.

My hand lies open on my book
two rings tell my doubly married tale:
husband and husband of my secrets
at home with kids.
          Later I tell him, my double husband, about you.
He says Tweed, where I woke, was where his grandfather
caught frogs in nets to sell to rich Americans.
legs twitch in Tweed as bus slows
stir
No harm

to you, to me, nor to the woman who touches your back with
sliding hand at stop past Tweed.
You smoke a pipe, Mr. Check Shirt. Through grey glass your
body I observe:
   long and flat. I like the way you move.
I like the way you sit with me again,
imagine your whole skin pressed on mine:
submission or surrender.
I like this silent talk between us with these curve-bound
pressures.
In Ottawa, I close book, comb hair, and turn:
Sunglasses, flash grin.
I knew you knew.

My sister, single, says it was Safe because I'm Married.
flower fire on thigh

chrysanthemum awareness opening
absolutely ordinary
beginner's mind
enforced
unforced
unfierce
you-man flowing outward into the world.

a close observer would see nothing
inside it shakes with life
and movement skin to skin:
your arm, my chest wall, my arm: a warm 3-D puzzle,
pieces big for child-size hands
in case God is clumsy.

-- Toronto to Ottawa, April, 1990.

Question

Would God do this for Dorothy -- shake out this flock of birds like silk,
winged caucus turning once twice three times against the golden mountains,
       light catching on underwings?
"No," John would say, "It's not that personal, the God-force, to arrange a private message just for you."
Four five six times, Birdmind turns turns, dark and flashing,
       the sky lit with blue.

Some Radical Animals

Animals are pets or wild.

Wild animals don't like to be written about.
Distant bears don't cross the mountain meadow.
They don't like our smell.

Wild animals I know:
insects snakes, and birds.
If you are there, the animals are no longer wild.
Raccoons at Long Beach are working on becoming pets,
begging and looking cute at campsites.

Then there are the city animals:
raccoons again, lolling on the grape on Easter Sunday
crows hopping black patterns, blitzing heads on the lime tree
street, leafy squirrels, pigeons.
City animals are adept at human meaning.

And there are zoo animals -- melodramatic in their melancholy.
Each one's suffering is real to her.

Animals have religion, a yeasty brew of what they think they
know and what might protect their lives.
This is what they believe:
            to look on human is to be doomed, corrupted, shamed,
and stunned.
            And shunned.
They have secret purification rites for this.
They've built kingdoms hard guarded by squirrels, crows,

pigeons, and raccoons
who've relinquished wildness
and are not yet pets.
Cuteness is their punishment, their life-long curse, their karma I
suppose.

"Submit to your higher power," counsel gentle wolves at night.
But Coyotes refuse cuteness, attack children in suburbs,
tricksters having it both ways, trafficking in human garbage.
Loping up the dark street, skinny shadows sinister.

Some radical animals want to kill humans, wipe out the
    human race.
They cite as heroes whales who in desperation crush
    human bones
        in murky human pools.
Fundamentalists rail at elder whales who loll in human nets,
        sweetly believing humans can learn.
"Optimists,"
"Fools," they bandy back and forth.
"They'll never change," radicals bray
        in mountain meetings. "The humans have to die,"
But they do not prevail and it is not just tactics.

The Lesbians of Trout Lake

are beautiful &
have healthy funny dogs.
I want to make love to them
(the women, not the happy dogs)
and to the men with big legs, stretching.

The path with its rhythmic
springy ups and downs,
        undulating,
seems to move like a woman's body
responding to a gentle hand,
accompanied by a concord of
        ululating ducks.

The girl dogs mount the boys,
        indiscriminate, ecstatic,
then splash joyously into trouty lake
to bark at fish
and ghosts of fish.

The seasons undulate:
grey, green, deeper green
the willows howl
and yellow flag, buttercup and water lily, sudden yelps of
yellow
then green again.
We walk around around the springy path
We are so sexy.

Bhoddisatva

The city is holy. Around and around the city, dripping oil,
treasuring wilderness, bearing beloved sacks of salty water.
Ernest in Safeway says it's Bhoddisatva energy. Too much of
that going on, I say. The city is holy. He's going out already,
hands free, grocery done, writing calling. I'm still going in,
wrestling boys, cart, energy: all things rough to the hands. No
time to find out how to spell what he said, just do it, breathing
all the time. If I remember: Bhoddisatva won't enter the
kingdom of heaven 'til Every
    Body can.
Later handfuls of ivy, kids pulling wildly with me, breathing
wet air.
Start where you are.
The city is holy.

Two: Aa

... a response to The Scarlet Letter by Nathaniel Hawthorne.

"She assured them too, of her firm belief, that, at some brighter period, when the world should have grown ripe for it, in Heaven's own time, a new truth would be revealed, in order to establish the whole relation between man and woman on a surer ground of mutual happiness."

1. The Hussy

My name is Hester
I walk in woods and by the shore,
my daughter at my hip
never ever meeting him
I do make sure.

Words rattle down the cliffs:
Pang.
Pang was one of your favourites:
as in "the pang that rankles after it".
May Pang: John Lennon's forgotten woman in Los Angeles.

Shame:
another good one.
You work with light, and shame lights up my face.
Shame, shame.

His voice went right through me:
"tremulously sweet, rich, deep, and broken".
That broken note, how it touched me down in the deep deep
shameful place.
You never wrote about what that felt like
and what we did
and where we did it
and only wrote that we said once that we were consecrated to
each other
You never wrote about whether I sat in later years in the
sunlit church
and watched the virgins thrilling to his voice.

You never showed the inside of that chapel, how the light fell.
You were better with exteriors: the light in the forest, the
burdock, and the solemn brook.

There was so much touching of the letter.
They all seemed free to touch and trace and point
My breast, my body's no body's body but my own.

My horrid husband the worst of all:
"he laid his long forefinger"
You never wrote, but it was clear, how cold that finger felt
        on skin.
I shuddered. It was sin.
I mean: to be touched so and allow it ever.
I paid the price.

Why did I stay in that place?
I could have flown.
There was the murmur on my skin,
a chance of that.
If he walked on cliffs, I took the hidden path.
If he dropped down to shore, I kept above.

You never wrote down how it felt:
his chest and shoulders how they felt on me
his hands in my hair.
The tender murmur on my skin.

I did the best I could
the loops and stitches of my life

embroidered;
did the best I could
hid my hair,
embroidered with small stitches
and dreamed of speech.

You said I had an Oriental love of gorgeous beauty.
I stitched Pearl's crimson tunics
the governor's gloves
and ruffs and finework
(all save the wedding work)

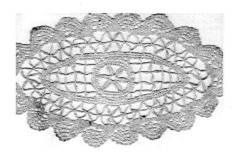

I stitched a way of listening,
      a wisdom.
I worked alone, my baby underfoot.

And you, Mr. Reverend Arthur Dimmesdale,
I want an extra measure.
three times you denied us in public
Arthur Peter, Reverend Dimmesdale
You gave your final mesmerizing sermon,
highstepped right by us, then
your words electric
I thrilled again, and still,
I thrilled:

their plaintive touch upon the human heart.

I was ready to start the whole thing over,
scratch cake bake from the beginning
the whole man-woman thing.
But I had no words, no voice,
was silenced into secrets, pressed
shut,
my stitches fine.

"What is the A for, Mummy, what?"

A is for apple
      and angel
      and able

A is for acceptance
      Thy will, not mine, be done
A is for Arthur
      and Author, who knew more than he said,
and said so much in
      fantastic flourishes of gold thread.
The A was on the heavens, a sign, a portent strange and drear
      the least lit light in the whole glowing tale.
A is for angel
      and able
      and

●

2. Three months in the dark of prison

My name is Pearl
      I glow unearthly
      I blink in sunlight and flicker.
On the darksome floor I glow,

"an absolute circle of radiance."
My mother surrounds me
I try to make her go away
I fling flowers,
sticky burdocks
at the A
AA
AAA
She has another name.
I call her A.
She never flinched
or flickered once.
The letter A glowed improved upon her breast,
fresh burdock green instead of scarlet.

"Yes mother," said the
child. "It is the letter A.
Thou has taught me it in the
horn-book."
She never flinches but she's never really there,
always looking out to where the path bends,
the cliff runs along the shore.
the minister with his sore picked A,
Her Arthur scratching at his chest in some dream of hidden
shame.

Then she met him that day in the forest:
moss, leaves, brook eddies, black depths, and
sparkling sand.
A wolf nudged me from behind
head against my hip
fur rough against my hand,
although all who heard later declared that beyond belief.
The wolf, she said to let it go.

"Preach, write, act!" my mother shouted then,

shaking out her lovely hair.
I was so
scared. I could hear across the brook.
"Preach, write, act."
I made her pin the A back on.
I washed and washed away his kiss.
I was so scared: a kiss in the woods is different, awful.
Don't preach write act.
Mrs. Higgins screeched, "You'll ride with me!"
The wolf said, "Let it go,"
and pressed her head against my palm.
At first I wouldn't listen, then
in the market place I kissed him,
Indians and pirates all around, the wild brought in.
I kissed and became a human child.
I watched my father die
and let it go.

I did not stay in that blackened place
Nor was I the
      Angel
      nor Apostle
of my mother's creed,
not I the prophetess
      of the baked from scratch cake
      of man and woman,
not lofty, pure, and beautiful
not I the one to speak her faith.
Though I listened well, and did believe,
in my flickering way.

●

3. The perverted healer

My name is Roger Chillingworth, or Mr. Prynne,
        never mind, I've had so many names.
She didn't care for me; I should have let her go.
I wandered with the Indians, happy enough,
the purple coneflower, pippesawa.
I studied where the world was fresh with life.
I should have let her go.

You said, Nathaniel, author:
"A writhing horror twisted itself across his features,
like a snake."
And you made me out to be a devil,
the dark man, sucking life out of the minister,
a sinner, it's my shame.
I did let her go. But I may have been a lover of the man,
I kept so close.
A huge draught of valium and herbs I shall not name
one noon I gave.
I crept in and touched his gently rising chest.
I guess I loved him in my way.

Why did I stay in that dismal place?
To be near that voice, that resonating chest,
to hate, to hate with all my love and fear.
My visage going sooty with the smoke.

They said perhaps I made the A,
Arthur's A.
He hid.
She wore her A so proudly.
But no, he was doing what he could himself.
The teeth of remorse,
chewing.
I didn't touch his chest again.
She wondered what poisonous shrubs start up beneath my hand,
black herbs on tombstones.

Indeed everything was poison at the end.
She tried to take him; I countered, holding fast.
He got away, the only way he could, at last.
I followed soon enough.

But once before I died, I walked out a day with Indians
to learn whatever came.
I stood listening, scarcely hearing, deep rumbling words,
in a language not my own.
The healer lifted leaves and spoke and spoke
a crowd had gathered round.
Then one pulled back. A snake.
The man talked on.

Of all the wild things I have met,
I've feared a snake the most.
But this time, I stood my ground.
A small gold red and yellow serpent climbed
green-veined and furry comfrey,
tasting with its tiny tongue.
I stood and stared,
Hello snake.
I was not afraid.
Soon after that I died.

I held him with my love, my rage, my herbs,
my blackened weeds.
But I was only human, sinned against.
And someday they will say there is another way.
I wait too for the Angel, the Apostle
who will speak
and hold not secrets,
hers or mine.
We shall all be free and
        my A turn green upon my chest.

Three:
Haibun Practice

08/12/00

Foggy morning. Water drops shining in street light. Memories of last writing class hanging, like wool blanket with drops of water hanging on surface, not wetting through. This idea of writing a Haibun a day as practice: up rises desire in the form of titles, publishing. 52 Haibun for the Millennium and grand ego thoughts. Throw them behind you. Can you do it to be present to the moment if you are writing in your head? Throw it behind you. Dog walks close, off leash, perhaps afraid of losing me in the fog. I take it as friendliness and speak warmly to her.

Do it for the Beloved.

09/12/00

In writing class blonde wings of hair and rolling laugh
Catherine asks, Do I really want people to know in my poem
that my father's a doctor? Strange question, I think, my face
shows. Because working class people might read and reject
because of my life of privilege. Inside I laugh. Doctor's
daughter, DD, we used to joke, my sisters, other DD's – a life of
service rather than privilege, of responsibility, and super-caring.
Then I say, "I used to." Used to hide where I was from, yes.
But now I think: This is all I have to give. I open ugly rippled
hands to Catherine of the lovely laugh. This.

One time in this skin, live it to the edges.

10/12/00

Breakfast with Helen at the Mokka Café. My hair all grey since
I saw her last. Sharing stories, how poetry slides to
disassociation. Monkey Mind asks about publishing. Orange
walls pleasing, feet cold. Two hours of Helen, intense: rich red
scarf wound below sincere face, upstanding grey shock hair, her
tic: "should I say?" said only once. Stand up to brightness,
surprise of other people, roomful of stories, coffee machines,
traffic. November rains disappeared and now December's. How
we enjoy this Global Warming, this cold brightness. She gives
me The Gift by Hafiz. We don't fight.

Each one has her own note in the song.

11/12/00

Garbling herbs at the kitchen table. Miles Davis on the player
like a rainy night. December sun streaming in. Peppermint
heady. Today the twenty-fifth anniversary of the December
defeat of the British Columbia socialists after just three years.
That night distressed at CBC in the Hotel Vancouver, taking
results by phone, wearing a leather mini skirt. Same me, same
wearing out body.

Then I didn't know the word joy.

12/12/00

Small Thai restaurant, watery delicious dishes in silver bins.
Woman serving with big lipstick out past her lips. Push away
rice and sit with jasmine tea and hear this behind: "He keep me
in. He don't let me go out by myself. I go out by myself big
trouble." I mishear: "He free me like a bird," and in the moment
before hearing right (he feed me like a bird) see her flying away
from his prison needs. Turn to see who speaks, the dark haired
smiling woman with the harried lips. Fly fly I want to call. She
is serving someone else. Lips weigh her down.

We flap slowly against gravity, free and yet falling.

13/12/00 & 14/12/00
Storm in the family and then sick with wicked flu. Shivering under blankets and quilts, afraid to move. Finally up for hot water bottle and throw up too. Family meeting at bedside with kids about confiscated tv. Some days just gritty and grotty cold and grey. Pumpkin on the edge of compost the only brightness. Cold.

Offering these kinds of days and doing my best.

15/12/00

Night banging the house, battering doors, trying to get in. I am the only "I" in the house awake, responsible, holding it all together. "I" not in control of the wind. The responsible "I" from next door, large white guy, is out walking the path in pyjama shorts, jacket over bare chest, checking the gate. In each house one "I" awake checking, holding our breath while the night bangs around, watching the wind in the trees, hurricane gusts. Dog and cat hiding. Blowing ice. Comes day with its many obligations: icy pickups money talk copying teenage soothing shiny paper expensive ribbon shopping cats teen soothing cooking dressing party obligation. Bad band and husband's flitting. Then snow again on ice. Car sideways slippery ballet on Eighth Avenue roaring clutch and pushing pushing then steady all the way home on Broadway, street lines covered with snow. Oh safe home. Safe. Minutes later just walking the dog feet gone shoulder hard on concrete ice. Collarbone broken or cracked.

Pay attention to the frequency on which signs are given.

16/12/00

Morning hospital quiet. Yesterday crazy they say. Waiting for doctor, for X-ray, for sling, for painkillers, waiting and quiet, meditating, okay. Chinese children with coats skipping, and across in a room a man moaning and bellowing vomiting and writhing, feet tied to the bed. He is I and I him, his pain mine, mine his. Meditating on a dream of fleeing, driving fast through people like him trying to stop me. Mine his, his mine. I get it.

In the dream, women in saris were showing the way.

17/12/00

Winter jasmine yellow and budding in my bag on the bus.
Poverty in a double stroller. Kids fussing hungry. Fruit leather
from my bag. Today is Rumi's Death Day, a feast day. A Sheik
speaks: "If you face the sun with your mind, the shadows fall
behind. They run after you calling but they stay behind." And:
"This body is an animal. The mind is the stick with which we
stir in the garbage searching." Asian forest quiet through
windows in dark afternoon. Ice gone almost everywhere. Peace
at home.

Nothing lasts, not the sickness, the peace, not the broken
collarbone. Not anything.

18/12/00 & 19/12/00 & 20/12/00
Preparing for Potlatch. Clipped in to the collective hard. No
escape. House clean, purified for the festival of abundance.
Matter dense, abundant, preparing. Giving is a letting go of
matter, your matter, not mine. Washing people, cupboards,
floors. The soft clean silk of my mother-in-law's hair. Teenage
lanky helping, getting it for the first time, about doing it right.
Broken collar bone aching.

If you can't love it, let it go.

24/12/00

Black leaves flap on crowns of two winter bare trees against winter grey sky. Christmas dread: work, people, hours, food, work. In memory: "Every moment perfect," sings Swami Jill the Yoga teacher, in pink or orange or yellow pants, sun on our faces. Dread lifts, crows lift into wind.

Like a dog left alone, past howling, this heart in winter sometimes.

26/12/00

Density intensity bright colours in grey light. Plowed through it, every moment perfect. Addiction crowding round the car of my life. A short binge harder to come back from than abstinence. Hafiz: "When you speak of shame you leave the tavern." Stay with us the perfect fabric of God's gown. Driving fast to outrun addiction. Need to stop and look and find my way. Women in saris will help me. Do.

Try to let desire rise up and fall away.

28/12/00

Slack water between seasons, slow swirl of days: mild bright. Red willow sticks at the lake, ice on puddles, city shining in early twilight, eyes straining for light. Sleeping a lot, bones healing, drinking good wine, watching bad TV. Not writing, not cooking, not cleaning, not doing laundry, not meditating. One son's quick funny smile from the couch with the cat. The other's extravagant gift of gratitude and bony hugs. Slow days pass quickly in this marriage and the tide rises and quickens soon enough.

We leave the tavern of the friends when we speak of wasting time.

01/01/01

Binary little row of numbers the new millennium brought in in a foreign place with blue green red yellow fire cascading off a tower with three human beloved ones in the dark below, crazy people all around and angry, a cascade of feelings over the days. Short sleep and don't erase anything on the train click clack: clear day shining on Puget Sound missed the Peace Arch. If there is no dualism 01 01 the universe is not binary 01 01 then there is no foreign land 01, though it seems in that place there is more metal on men's hips, more metal in the cities 01. Why be mystical about numbers? 01 01 01.

If I was called to go to live there, Love, would you come?

02/01/01

Potlatch over and we're empty again, tree in the back still smelling noble pine, cards gathered, fridge clear. Potlatch is cleansing because it's all offered, all of it, the feast, the excess, the heaviness of family and matter, cheques to charity, chocolates to the Lookout, addiction dreams (addicted people running after my car, throwing themselves in front), reawakened cravings crawling inside skin. In dream: alcoholic friend with soft curly hair who smells of marijuana and offers it and the place at the table in the tavern where there is no chair for me. All gone. Gate Gate Paragate.

Money is energy they say. I'm trying to understand.

03/01/01

Write memo to children and food in fridge. I'm packed in my head and flying tomorrow. Shoes one pair, two pairs, three pairs, travel light, take care with packing. So hard to believe that time isn't real when this time I have waited for has finally arrived. And though the sky is dark now at 3:15 it will get lighter day by day and they say the world has a fever why all this weird weather. Coming earth changes. What is in store? Practising equanimity.

Everyday darkness.

04/01/01

The shoulder on which I turn to you, Love, is the sore one,
broken, much better now. In darkness I rolled to you last night
but couldn't stay, it hurt. Can't unlock the door for you driving
and can't roll to you in bed. "We could change sides," I said.
We laughed. After this many years, lying this way, in this
rumpled bed, one of us would fall or bump our head. So we
touch hands and wish each other well for this journey and let
the energy sink back. Today I'm off above clouds, Love, and
through turbulence while you still sleep.

Grateful for this gentle elastic love.

05/01/01

Morning meditation in the golden hall. Meditaters like one
beast, settling, coughing. Clearing noses, softening. Then many
images: the heart opens like a … but they are all gone.
Turquoise behind eyes. And this remembered: heart is a seed,
praying for a great bird to pluck and carry off. Twitching with
joy.

Passion is long patience.

06/01/01

What should we do so that the Friends don't have to wait so long? What should I do? Hate to keep anyone waiting. I'll do anything: write news releases for the new energy, travel to far lands, meditate 23 hours a day. What? What should I do? Suppressed questions sink down, joy rises up. Joy in different boxes says Rumi. In this one fish and rice for lunch, in that a dog's happy nose on the beach. Here the pop of seaweed tangled in mystic cones, there sunlight on golden tangle of hair, stranger's hair, a friend's. Joy in all these crazy boxes and questions like an itch. No my dear we don't do anything. Oh.

Today was the Feast of Epiphany.

07/01/01

It's not that I don't want to leave, though I don't. It's not that I'm still waiting for that breaking of Oneness across my body, though I am. It's not that I feel suddenly alone, though I do. The wooden floor that creaked when I came to meditate sounds the gentle shuffle of feet going. The golden curtain that framed a cascade of glorious words trembles. Drum echoes, an orchestra of sound produced on one stretched skin and one curve of wood, hang still in the air. I've been here a long time now. I feel at home. It's not that I'm afraid to go on. I'm not. It's just if I sit here with my heart open a moment and write these words, it's just that I do.

This is a prayer for the Beloved to play me like that drum.

11/01/01

This imperfect work: like a leaf with insect holes. Four days since I wrote and last night at writing school I spoke of my Daily Practice. The Beloved laughs and beckons come come. It's leaf mold maybe, this holey practice curled on the ground, mulch for something. Meanwhile my head full of angels weeping.

Ninety-nine names and the only word that comes to mind is Why?

17/01/01

Peat moss underfoot, a springy step, advising others every day. Knowing, how not to tell, restraint is called for. My heart open, the mouth knows what to say. Is this ego? If ego, can I let it go? Throw it behind me like a striped rock into the ocean making a wish. Wishing for love on a star and here it is, here it is.

So grateful.

18/01/01

Today I am invisible, a grouchy brown tree with a black hat.
Black pickup truck turns into my path driving. Later in the same
place almost plowed by a white car. At least the driver puts his
hand to his mouth in mock horror. Next crosswalk speeding
black car doesn't even see me. Dog invisible too, black fading
into the pavement, squished. Back to old ways, doing things for
people out of obligation, feeling overwhelmed overtaken and
not sure what I really should be doing. The whole morning a big
waste of time looking up e-mail addresses for the school and
this is definitely not a poem.

So you see.

22/01/01

A child makes a boat from chunks of wood, unsleek and satisfying. This writing is just big chunks of wood. The author, teaching, says, "You have to think about who's going to ride in the boat." In my mind it's sleek and fast skimming the Everglades and yet it comes out clunk clunk clunk. Slow too. The couch calls, "Come come though you've broken your vows a thousand times, come," doing a soft impersonation of Rumi. Alas I fight it. Stay here. Fingers going clunk clunk clunk.

The thousand and first time the boat might start.

29/01/01

Talking with poets makes the mind keener. How I know is, not talking with poets now is duller. Novelists talk about advances and audience. Poets talk about crows and readers. In the tops of the tallest wet willow on the east side of Trout Lake, thousands of crows all cawing obsessed with their story. Not sweeping and upset, no hawk or eagle to buzz. Just sitting yakking, loud and ridiculous. "Maybe I'll be a poet when I grow up," they caw. Crows are a sign of the Divine.

If only the heart was as keen as the mind.

29/01/01

Dull Monday, rainy or the leftovers. Deliver kids and expensive equipment. Stormy grocery store resentment. Back over the bridge something pushing the van. Down into the city and the day explodes with wind and sunshine. Drop the groceries and get the dog. Crows all out of the golden-branched willows. Eagle ruckus right overhead. Big swells on the lake and puddles rippled up with wind. Seagulls ripple up the blue of sky chasing eagle. Everything bright.

The hard practice is to be as present to the gray and groceries as to the bright exploded day.

06/02/01

A man walks up the street through grey trees by grey fence with
tree shadows and sun stripes playing across his grey body. Put
on glasses to see better but it's worse. Cat this early morning as
I tried to meditate racing up and down stairs, pushing around
clacking bit of plaster from the ceiling where Chuck cut holes to
pull knob and tube wiring to replace with good solid Lurex.
Knobs and tubes old and greasy dusty, old wires twisted and
brittle. My thoughts greasy and dusty, meditation twisted and
brittle.

Why depressed again after all these months of lightness?

11/02/01

The way a dog picks up a scent, is turned by it, you can tell
there's a quilt, a weaving of smells in the air, invisible, three-
dimensional, unknowable to us with our shoddy human noses.
And journalist friends who scorn my theological bent, what are
they smelling with, what missing? Would I be right to say to
Codi, wheeling on a smell and zig zagging across the savannah
at Trout Lake, "Hey you. There's nothing there. Cut it out.
You're deluded." I might say, "Silly dog, pulled around by
smells," or "Come on we have to go." This morning in bath
remembered: glossy book we used to read kids about a juggler:
"Fool of God". Am I?

All these golden balls in the air.

20/02/01

In John's vision, the bear falls down gracefully onto all fours, safe by the ocean, seagull wheeling helpfully overhead. And, through dark portal of dream, I remember crawling, hands and knees, effortful, uphill, along the path by the castle. That castle appears over and over. That and the recurring dream of being married, being married. I was making love to my freedom, and now trying to understand what it would mean to be free. It's so abstract, not about marriage, or not this marriage. Then this: dark dogs loping along on their wrist bones.

If not about marriage, then what?

21/02/01

Declare a meditation day, calendar yawning Emptiness. Phone rings and rings, every call important: a death, my sister-in-law's mother, then Helen caught: her stories about Palestine in oppression rejected, another sister-in-law whose hips ache. So the practice is being present. Teenager home from school at loose ends, all loose around the house. Feed him French fries and chicken and no nagging about jobs and school. So the practice is being present. And he's off skateboarding into the sunlight before I've paid for the sandwich. Other son home glowing from some unspeakable girl thing lays his head on my leg while we argue about tattoos. Being present while he talks about cars one of the hardest things I do now. Ego clamouring for recognition: you do this presence thing so well. Throw it behind like the dog's found bone, greasy with saliva and sharp.

Always going back for those delicious bones.

(Here the Haibun practice breaks off.)

Four:

Bittersweet:

45 Haibun for My Father

1.

I was the first person ever whose father died. He told me he was
dying driving to blood transfusion. Matter of fact, 88: "I'm
worried about Mum." Me. wildly: "We'll take care of her." I
was the first ever to carry this stone in my belly. In obituaries
fathers died. Friends' fathers died or were dead. But they never
felt this very stone. I'd have heard. There'd be commotion,
uproar, feature articles. Fathers die; people carry on. But me,
driving the city round and round, through blossom canopy,
dappled shade, forthysia, light rain, carrying father and stone to
transfusion, haemotologist, transfusion again, unique,
preoccupied, deep with the stone.

We fear death because we don't know anything else.

2.

My father's body stopped making blood. My mother suffered cognitive loss, Alzheimer's or Vascular Dementia. Her sad questions repeated and repeated. My sisters and I cared for Mum in her home for eight months while Dad was in and out of hospital. He died. Three months later she went into a care home. That's the short version. What follows is the long version. It took about a year in the world's time.

All we know about Reality is this short trajectory in a body.

3.

Ah! It came to me: stone in the chest is self-pity. In Yoga: "I bow down to Thee for the removal of my self-pity": stretch up, bow down, on knees, stretch out (purple mat), lift hands linked, cobra, child, back on heels, up again, ending prayer: "I offer this asana to the Divine." Stone melted and was gone.

The little self stalls and balks, says no, doesn't know.

4.
July 26, 2002. Getting ready for bed, step from bath to phone.
Transfusion and something gone wrong up the coast. Sister
called an ambulance. Go. Thirty-five minutes to last ferry. Go.
Go. Go. Speeding against my slow paced nature, breathing the
name of God, lavender still in the air. Highway in darkness.
Phone from the ferry. The first time we thought he was dying.

Flying on the name of God.

5.

Is he dying? Should get everyone on airplanes? Sister-nurse in
Arctic and brother country-crossing with kids? Doctor says no,
speaks enthusiastically about staying alive. Reels off blood
counts, haemoglobin, phytocils. Try this, try that. Now I know:
he was nowhere near death. He said he was dying. I said, "Are
you afraid?" He said, "No. What's there to be afraid of?" I said,
"I've come to believe we're souls." He smiled, "You mean we
just go on?" "Yes. On into the Love." He smiled, radiant,
lovely, morning light streaming into the ward. Lines rayed out
from his eyes, lovely. A long way to go yet.

These miraculous bodies we've been given are tough.

6.

He was the photographer. Pictures of sea shining to dark horizon. Telephoto children mandalas, intent on sand castles. Red boat shining on blue. Birds: eagles, sandpipers, woodpeckers, heron, eagle diving. Making a gift of it all to us. Photos of him show work gloves hanging from resting hands. Work his meditation. Humming his tuneless hum around the garden. Summer years: dirt, compost, water, tomatoes, wood chopping, photography. A sensualist. The last summer: home from hospital, down to essential sun on face and shins. Binoculars to hand.

Sensual people use the holy names often, but they don't work for them.

7.

Two summers earlier, he turned up two brittle envelopes: his war photos, cleared by himself, the censor, senior medical officer. Before battles: men, vehicles, tents. Never spoke of war before, but now sat, slowly shuffling, remembering. "This was Normandy." "This the Scheldt. Attached to British Commandos there." Spoke slowly, carefully turning each tiny picture. How he defied a major who ordered vehicles washed in gasoline. How this man was the sergeant, a good man. "Wonder what happened to him?" Long marches, drugged to stay wake. His ambulance. His motorcycle. Mud. How he forgot to vaccinate himself, got sick. How bombers flew over, some men ducked below tables. "You couldn't really do that. You had to just keep working." Not teaching, just saying. Summer sun set pink and blue over still water as he spoke.

Stoicism is the graceful acceptance of what is there before you.

8.

Summer's end. Sister-nurse could stay a month and keep them
there in ocean, sky, sun, trees, birds, passing eagles, starlight,
beach and moon. Father's face lights. Imagine September sun
on shins. But mother freaks. A collapse as one by one we give
in. Led by him, we give in to her. Staring down at our bare feet
on the hot wood of the deck. She cries, gets her way. What is it?
Fear? Home they will go on Labour Day. Home to the city
where she imagines she has a social life, imagines she goes to
studio, takes yoga, sees friends. All gone, the golf friends
mostly dead. We all know, save her, this is his last summer.

Each time in a body is finite – so hard to accept.

9.
Driving to transfusions we spoke of her through tunnels of
blossom, and fall changed leaves. Spoke as though we were
parents and she the troubled child, spoke of my childish mother.
Why could she never believe she was loved? When he had
ulcers and her sister ulcers too, they lay above and talked from
bed to bed while spouses drank below. Her sister said their
mother was cold, pushed them away, planned divorce, spoke to
her child about it. This elegant grandmother of mine, giving tea
parties, welcoming grandkids, was cold and unreliable in her
love. We spoke of her.

What is passed from mother to child, what karma from life to
life?

10.

Who cooks? Eight years before, Mum broke hip in frantic fall;
Dad learned to cook. Now she can't. She says, "I can; I just
don't want to." Burns toast, boils kettles dry. Believes she
cooks. No one argues. Doctor says, "What did you cook?"
Can't remember. Sisters brother come, cook, leave meals. All
summer sisters cooked. Now father cooks slowly, slowly
grilling lamb chops, steaming vegetables. She believes she
cooks. They eat little teeny slow meals on trays. Both skinny.
Can't hear each other any more.

Love in these frail bodies survives somehow.

11.

Sister-nurse will soon fly north. Dad insists she go, not wait for him to die. A farewell dinner. "Spare no expense," he says. So a bright private room, flocked wallpaper, polished round table, fois gras, red and white wine. He used to be big, carving, joking, ordering wine. Hard work now to sit, to listen. Hard work for Mum. But love spins the room. For two hours, this is what love feels like, spinning, holding us aloft. November 22, 2002. Last time all together like this.

Love spins at a higher frequency.

12.

December, leg bleeding. Call from the bathroom: "Can you help me?" Piling on bandages, pressure. Won't stop. No platelets, no clotting. Wad of bandages under pant leg. Tea at Janet's, elegant old people. Good silver. Bleeding still after, in the dark afternoon, stain on good tan pants. Call sister nurse to dress it, then she's back to Arctic nursing, to medivacs, darkness, always on call. I'm the on-call daughter for the next four months.

Suffering is inevitable on this plane because matter is so dense.

13.

December afternoon walking. Dark dog romps in wet snow.
Under willows we round the dark lake. Something comes, wild.
Near dusk straining for silvery light. Something: frail old man
flailing, dark against snow, slipping, lurching. "Do you want
help?" Takes offered arm. But lurching, his weight too much.
Slipping. Both of us will fall. No English or no words. Others
help. "Hold him here while I carry him here." To picnic bench.
911 on my father's cell. Small crowd circles. Someone gathers
my gloves and hat thrown down. Someone knows someone who
speaks Chinese, "He says everything fine. Not to bother."
Everything not fine. Old man wet along one side, dark clothes
darker, he's fallen. Can't walk, can't say where he lives,
shivers. Sit thigh to thigh to warm. Paramedics pick their way
across snow, pick out his wallet, say they'll warm him, bully
him into ambulance. Look askance at me, a busybody. All this a
harbinger. Patient dog lying waiting. We go home. A harbinger.

Things happen first on the inner planes and then on the outer.

14

Christmas 2002. Drive fragile elders packed in sleeping bags out freeway south to sister's boyfriend's house. House in wet trees, creek below. Turkey, stuffing, cranberry, sweet inquisitive dog, candles, kids. But for Dad, the house, the straight trees, the creek nearby, sparkling in wet sunlight. He sees my sister's happiness sparkling and straight after a long dry spell. He sees the trees, the creek. It pleases him. Last Christmas here on earth. And home again well before dark. They tire easily.

The days are short.

15.

January 6, 2003. His hands swollen and painful, red splotches and pain moving up his arms. Won't call doctor. Sister-nurse from North: "You're a stubborn old goat." I sleep on wretched lumpy fold out couch, ready. Call in the night: "Can you help?" Up in a second, alert in darkness and sudden brightness. Get behind, hold him as he walks. Awkward. Difficult. Bones, and skin moving over bones. Body melting away. Hold ribs while he pees, my shoulder against his bony back. Calm. Realizing: I'm holding my skinny father while he pees. And slowly back to bed. Morning: mother strangely lucid, "We should call an ambulance." Calmly: dress, eat breakfast, call ambulance. The end of normal, all strangely calm.

Stay in the moment and there is no time for fear.

16.

In Emergency waiting. His lips dry, face skin flaking, everything dry. Vasoline and ice chips. Waiting. Mum in a chair beside. Sixty years married, prepared to sit through anything. He's trying to say something, voice a rasp, a whisper. Lean close to hear. "Starbucks," he says. "And doughnut." Screw twenty years of careful diabetes. And when delivered, tasted, "Mmm." Appreciation. Sensual.

To be alive is to be in this body, tasting the world.

17.

Mum: doesn't drive, can't cook, doesn't know the year, the Prime Minister's name. In anxiety asking: what's going to happen? Over and over. Trying to stay in control where she's always been. Sits in the car while you shop for her groceries. Can still clothes shop, recognize and make a word joke, tell you to comb your hair. Her hair just grey fluff on her head. Skinny, size small and extra small. A librarian who loves books and words and can't read. Walks with a cane now, good for fending off friendly dogs, but not alone. Needs constant care.

I bow down to Thee for the removal of my impatience.

18.

Week 2 of wakeful nights on lumpy fold down couch. Dad in hospital; Mum can't be alone, is anxious, lights fires with damper closed and fills the room with smoke. Has never lived alone. Eighty-eight years. Sons need me too, call on the cell. Which way to turn? Sister-teacher to stay some nights. Make schedule. Husband books off, takes son to doctor, buys bed. Lumpy couch in our house now. It goes on and on.

I bow down to Thee for the removal of my impatience. Again.

19.
"I've been lying here thinking about food," Dad says. Mobility
gone. Mind clear, thoughts to food. Thin slices of rare roast beef
with gravy and drippings on bread with butter. French fries
crisp and golden. A thick milkshake. Steak and Kidney pie from
the Diner. Thick homemade pea soup. Pancakes with syrup and
butter. All these savoured in the hospital bed over weeks and
weeks of immobility. These and a few good jokes say I am
alive. Avid. Asks to see newspaper headlines then shakes his
head and drops the paper. War approaches in Iraq.

Visualize the world as One, place it in your heart, fill the world
with peace, remember it to God.

20.

Afternoon tear away like noisy velcro from Mum with hired woman. Sister-teacher coming later. Using the cell by roadside, taking calls, secretly trying to figure out care. Down through drug dealing men swirling on dirty sidewalk to Only Café, only remnant of old Skid Row, plain and poor, linoleum and thick white cups, a working place. What he wants today: fish and chips from the Only. Packed up to go. Back to hospital corner room. Sunset across the western city, church spires shining. He relishes golden greasy fish, thick potato chips, white bread, thick pats of butter, coleslaw in Styrofoam. A zesty feast. Alive. Sun on his face. Suddenly then: coffee spilled out, head thrown back, eyes roll. I call out. Hit panic button. Long seconds twitch and pass. He returns face flushed red. Appetite gone. Nurse with her blood pressure machine.

Simply to be in each moment.

21.

Music. Brother brings discman and Beethoven. But deep in music with earphones cutting out nurses, cleaners, moans, and street noise, his heart stops and tips him upside down. Heart stops and tips him. Upside down. Can't listen. Brother brings small wind up radio. Quality poor but street noise nurses cleaners, all the world there still. And news. War is starting, is going to start. "Crazy," he shakes his head.

Simply to be alive in the noise of each moment.

22.

Weeks in bed. Pacemaker in. Now time for physio, time to get
up. My mother urging, urgent, pushing. "You don't know
whether you can do it 'til you try." With two aides, he shuffles
up, great effort. "Remember the Normandy Roof," she calls out.
The Normandy Roof in Montreal where they danced, twirled,
flew through the summer night. He twirled her, hand on her
back. Her dresses shimmered and belled.

Now dinner jacket hangs thin and dusty at home, would fit him
again, patent leather shoes shiny and empty. He makes it from
bed to hall and barely back, gown crumpled and open over his
thinness.

Such a brief dance each time.

23.

Twenty hours away, off-duty, I step from elevator into blue grey weariness. Elevator to door handle seems a desert of blue-grey plastic weariness. Feet sinking in dimpled blue- grey plastic weariness. Sinking and lifting. Take breath, practise lifting voice in greeting. Impossible that the voice will lift. This passes. Door opens. Inside, a sister ready to get away, the sweetness of my mother, real and trying, carpet, food, fire, need. Voice lifts in greeting.

One day at a time, bow down to the circumstances of life.

24.

I dream that my mother is dying, getting smaller and smaller in my hands. Call 911. Family gather. Smaller and dying. Dream sister-in-law says, "Hold her like this." Hold her like this and her heart starts beating against my hands. Holding her beating heart in my hands. Wake up in their house my heart beating hard. So vivid: she must have died. Tiptoe in to her room to hear her sleeping quietly. No I see. I am holding her heart in my hands. In real life sister-in-law said, "She must be afraid."

Doing what I am doing to the edge of my skin.

25.
Geriatric medicine. Wheel chair to exercise, to physio. Man in next bed yelling at nurses. Everything slow. Time to organize wheelchair and walker for home. Time to organize care aides, home nurses. Time to get into routine with Mum. Dressing every day to go see him. Helping him into wheelchair, "Old man," he says, ruing it. "Does it come as a surprise to you, Dad?" Week after week. Then finally coming home.

We are not given to know what we are here for.

26.
March morning. He's home. Propped by pillows, dressed, pacemaker wound exposed, waiting for home care nurse and her dressing, he says, "I want you to plan a trip with John. I will pay." For when nurse sibling returns, when someone else can care for Mum. Hectoring. "Will you promise?" Can't see how we can leave our boys. Can't imagine going. But the idea takes hold. John's brother can stay with boys. Book a trip. Mexico easy, all inclusive. Still weeks and weeks away. Still caring twenty-four seven. He writes a cheque, satisfaction real, like when he has a good meal. "That's good then."

The gratitude attitude.

27.

Mum to Gerontologist now Dad is home. Driving rain and wind. Parking impossible. Umbrella blown and up long slow steps. There was an easier way but we didn't know. Mum scared and grouchy. Damp. Waiting. Can't name the Prime Minister, the year, the names of her grandchildren. Diagnosis Alzheimers. Then doctor to me: "You've come about memory, you'll be back about behavior." And to her, "You are a smart lady with memory problems." Mum happy.

Just stay in the fucking moment.

28.

The muffled world goes by. We are in a tunnel of illness and oldness. Driving here and there see blossoms, people walking, drinking coffee, at leisure. All just beyond possibility. One day at transfusion hospital, urgent carpenters work. Build new doors. Women with high heels and clipboards supervise. By day's end everything gone except us and our wheelchair. Next day our serene transfusion ward a secure SARS clinic. Screening tent in the parking lot. From upstairs as they transfuse, we watch the first patient come, face-masked, swarmed by cameras and questions, get back in car and drive away.

The world has many surreal games to play.

29.
Haemoglobin falling fast. Transfusion day one. Hours later back
to get him. Helping him dress, kneeling, one pant leg two pant
legs over the feet. He says, "I told the doctor I wanted to make
it till D. got home. Just say hi, then go. I don't think I'm going
to make it. These transfusions are a waste." Pull up his pants.
"Dad. Your quality of life is good. You're not in pain. You can
eat and enjoy your food." Fasten pants on skinny waist. "And
God knows, no-one in the world begrudges you the blood."
Nurse there suddenly around the curtain, hair in braids, face
sincere, "Speaking for the medical system, I have to agree with
that." Kneel again for shoes.

These bodies take us down and up and it all seems real.

30.

In and out of hospital again. Patched up. New wonderful
energy, alert and bossy. He walks Spanish Banks, ten yards and
sits on walker in sun. Excited, I propose drive and lunch, as in
days when they were parents intact, would come to get me and
drive me and lunch me and drive me home again, intact.
Brilliant spring sun, sea sparkling to Horseshoe Bay. But
getting into car he nicks hand. Skin thin. Bleeding and won't
stop. Bleeding all through lunch. Calamari. Bleeding. Refuse
home or hospital. Bleeding. "Don't fuss." Bleeding from the
inside, bleeding from outside. Learn a new word Maelena:
blood in stool, dark sticky stool. Bleeding. Hand keeps on
bleeding. Home nurses dress it, exotic wonderful dressings,
butterflies, expensive beauties. Bleeding for days and days.
Nurse-sister gone another three weeks.

These bodies a miracle, a mystery.

31.
Wheelchair in the back of car. Elders loaded. My muscles doing
the right things. A sense of rightness, of lifting the whole thing
properly. That this is right. All is well. All manner of things are
well. Load mother with cane, check seat belt. Lock brakes on
wheelchair, Dad into car, seatbelt, close door, fold up chair,
open trunk, lift chair, close trunk, into driver's seat. I can do all
this. My muscles know what to do. It is right. John holding the
fort at home: shopping, cooking, cleaning, taking care of boys,
still working. It is all okay.

You float along the river with your burdens floating beside you.

32.

Music again. Mum restless and anxious, harder for her when
Dad home. She consents to music for once. We eat to music, sit
afterwards, music washing over us Beethoven, Brahms. One
long CD: Bach, Mozart, Vivaldi. All the old hits packed into
one floating evening. Mum quiet, for once not insisting on her
own needs. Then help Dad to bed. "That was good," he says. It
was good.

This time in this world so short.

33.
Sister-nurse is coming home! Two days of travel. Three planes.
Four medivacs the last week. No sleep. Mum and I to airport to
meet her. Dad sitting up on couch at home. Slow-walking Mum.
Cart big bags. Home Guinness stout all round. Beer's been
chilling for a week for her. Dad to sister: "It's been a long four
months." He's animated, happy. I drive her home, come back.
Dad napping on couch. He doesn't get up. To Emergency that
night. Sent home. Emergency the next morning. He doesn't go
home again.

The human will is a mystery; it can hold together a tattered
human body.

34.

Pacemaker is infected and infection antibiotic resistant. Only one surgeon in the province can take it out and start again. In Coronary Care, waiting. Politely ask when it's going to happen. Nurse looks worried, says he's very low. She says he has orders on his chart to give CPR. Oh no. That's wrong. He wakes for a moment I ask. No. Wrong. Regular nurse gone. Call another nurse to witness. My father says, "No CPR." We're caught up in forces we don't understand. Doctors consult just out of earshot. Family gathers to wait. Another death watch.

Maybe the greedy ego likes all this drama.

35.

Wash hands in. Coronary Care Unit: glass rooms, long pale
curtains, monitors, steel sinks, folding toilets. Big family,
Indian, crushed into glass room across, woman wailing, spicy.
A death in the unit. Each room a little theatre. Brown family
giving lessons: this is how to deal with death: wailing, tearing
long silky garments. Here we sit in silence. Lines stutter green
across monitor dark. "Don't look; the monitor lies," say nurses,
who look. Lines stop. He clutches. Lines go. Eases, wakes a bit,
heart stopping wake-up. Gone for seven seconds, monitor says.
Sleeps again. Don't look at monitor. They come to turn and
wash him. Wash hands out. Dawn over parking lot.

Being in a body is a mystery.

36.

April morning CCU. Nurse: "He's low, may die today." Cell
phone in the ambulance bay, call everyone in. We're still asking
New Pacemaker? Doctors consult out of earshot. Sense this
from them: why can't they just let him go? Children and wife
ring the bed, all calm. Is this it? Clear space for doctor, defer.
Tall doctor at foot of bed speaks: "Sometimes people are tired
of it all, they don't want to keep going." Speaks ten minutes,
hands on bed rail as on podium, asks nothing, says only:
"Sometimes people are tired." Pager goes; he's gone. Siblings
to siblings across white bed, laugh, say, "Well I don't know." "I
guess it's not up to us anyway. It's up to the Big Guy." Sing:
"Go where you wanna go, do what you wanna do, with whoever
you wanna do it with." Everyone gone but me, I say, "Well Dad
what do you think?"

What would it be like just to surrender?

37.

"So Dad what do you think?" Sitting by his bed. He's still
awake. Doctor gone, family gone. "He makes a lot of sense. But
I don't want to do it at your expense." Repeat it. At your
expense. "You mean the trip?" "Yes. Promise that you'll go. No
matter what." A death bed promise to go away. Cornered. It's
what he wants. I promise. That night: green lines stutter and
stop and jerk him awake heart stopped, he sees me. "Are you
still here? You should go." Confused for a moment, for the first
and only time. That I should be on the plane I finally realize.
"Not til Sunday Dad. Still here for now."

Still here, in this body, for now.

38.

April evening CCU. Long light in the ambulance bay. Grandson
storms in crying. His life has been rocky, difficult. A big man
now, crying. "Grandpa. I'll miss you so much. I love you so
much." Loud, crying. Dad comes up, up from unconsciousness,
roused by this energy. Grandson leans in crying, talking.
Grandpa smiles, dry lips stretched across dentures that don't fit
his shrunken body. Smiles at grandson with his wild grief.
Smiles and smiles. Grandson turns to me and says, "I don't
know what else to say." "Talk about your memories. Fishing in
the red boat." Grandson says, "Remember Grandpa you took me
fishing in the red boat?" He smiles and smiles while Grandson
wails. Blows out again. Just in town for a night and gone. Back
one time to borrow money for the phone. And gone. Dad
doesn't die that night.

The river of life flowing fast here and wild.

39.

Doctors consult out of earshot. Suddenly they're doing the pacemaker. In and out of surgery and back on the other ward. These nurses thought he would die. Now he's back. The room next to the one where the seagull comes to the window sill. We're back in shifts, gathered around, bringing milkshakes. Doctor says never mind blood sugar. Eat anything. Bring bright flowers. Trees out the window. Moonlight on the bed. Still alive. Still alive.

The door between the worlds is open.

40.

Palliative now. New pacemaker in, infection still raging. Not whether, when, sooner rather than later. Driving east in April sun, a "free" afternoon, palliative care doctor on the cell. Bus driver brother on holidays, can be with father while he dies. Sister-nurse. We gather. Talk. While we gather and talk he gets physio for the first time this round. Up in a chair, hoisted by a sling. He comes awake. Mostly unconscious but when conscious, all there.

This soul in this body. This time.

41.

10 pm Thursday conference. Four siblings criss cross phone lines talking. What to do? Three at the 10 pm table. One home with Mum. Short energetic doc meets us to decide. He's working Emergency, pager going, working the phones. Try to talk through drug overdoses and falling blood pressure. Could: stop food, stop saline, stop antibiotic, stop blood. Not painful, just a gentle sliding away. Brother not ready. And still up to Dad. Go for a strange beer after, as if out on the town. Sunday to Mexico. He insisted. Everything is strange.

Drink the fine wine of life to the dregs.

42.

Saturday afternoon to hospital with John to say good-bye. Off to Mexico to honour our promise. Dad's up, still awake. I know this the last time I'll see him this time round. John thanks him for the trip. Dad says: "I'm very glad to do it for you." I to Dad: "You have a good trip." Kiss his dry lips and hug bony shoulders. Then in the hospital hallway weeping, John holding me. Weeping with the conviction of having been blessed. So blessed. All of us blessed by his life.

What a joy to be in these bodies here and now.

43.
Sunday flight. I promised to go. I went. Air-conditioned e-mail room. Everywhere else hot with ocean breeze. E-mail the morning swim in Caribbean, the phone number. Later sister says he smiled at swim before breakfast. Silly resort: swim up bar, all in, sweet drinks, absurd abundance. Grateful to rest, to walk the beach, to be with John. So strange to be here with hot and cold streams of sorrow and joy under crashing palm leaves and brilliant blue sea. Too windy to snorkel. Diving through waves.

Why are we here in these strange human bodies?

44.

Friday night this dream: I'm in a hospital ward. Nurses call us to his dying. (As they did so several times in life) I find him among many men, take his head in my hands, say, "We had a wonderful trip Dad." On waking tell dream to John, laugh, and say "I wonder what that's all about?"

Gratitude is balm to so many hurts and sorrows.

45.

"Bittersweet," The word comes up out of a quick deep sleep. Saturday night, leaving tomorrow. John still up, reading in a chair, says, "What?" "Bittersweet." Half hour later Mexican phone pierces dark. Fumble to answer. "He's gone." Mum and sister came into the room. He'd gone moments before. Mum says he waited for her; she touched his hand and he went. Sister said he may well have still been there. Death is when all movement stops.

This knowing: we are souls and these bodies are holy.

Epilogue: Embodiment

Embodiment

All the babies are crying on the Number 9 bus.
At Clark Drive, Beautiful Girl gets on, body swaying,
freckled breasts, belly below blue shirt smooth and
       round and brown,
hair long, resplendent, red.
Judging mind takes in: round hips, shadow of underwear in
       thin white pants.
Judging mind chatter: how could she show so much? Intrigued.

I close my eyes and wander in and out of vastness.

By Main St. she is old, and offered a seat by polite young men
in hip hop orange,
her hair chopped off and dry, boobs sagging in same faded and
worn blue shirt,
belly hanging over pants.
Judging mind turns away. How could she?

I close my eyes and wander, swaying, in and out of vastness.

By Granville she is stooped, body twisted, unshapely, face
pulled down by stroke and whiskered. She drools and cannot
feel it.
She stands uncertainly, stumbles.
Hands reach out to catch her.
Judging mind: pity.

In and out of vastness.

By MacDonald she is gone to spirit. This body time so brief, a
cross-town bus ride.

In and out. Vastness.
At Alma I get off the bus, walk five blocks to where ocean
touches city,
and swim again in deep delicious salt.